ICE HOCKEY LEGENDS

Martin Brodeur

Sergei Fedorov

Peter Forsberg

Wayne Gretzky

Dominik Hasek

Brett Hull

Jaromir Jagr

Paul Kariya

John LeClair

Mario Lemieux

Eric Lindros

Mark Messier

CHELSEA HOUSE PUBLISHERS

ICE HOCKEY LEGENDS

PAUL KARIYA

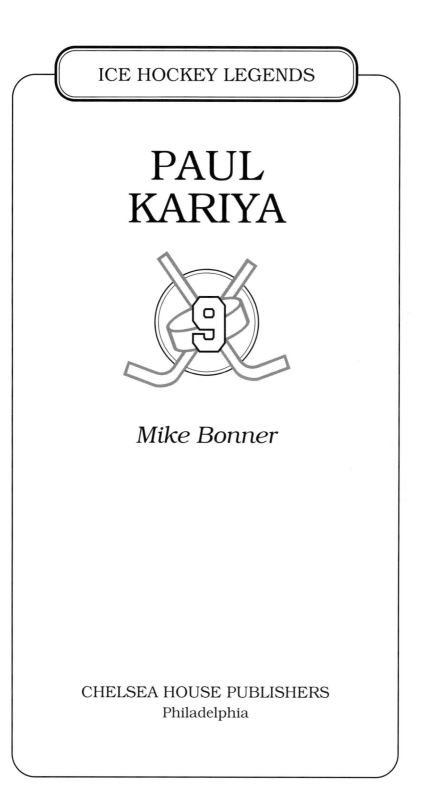

Mike Bonner

CHELSEA HOUSE PUBLISHERS
Philadelphia

Produced by P. M. Gordon Associates
Philadelphia, Pennsylvania

Picture research by Gillian Speeth, Picture This

CHELSEA HOUSE PUBLISHERS

Editor in Chief: Stephen Reginald
Managing Editor: James Gallagher
Production Manager: Pamela Loos
Art Director: Sara Davis
Director of Photography: Judy L. Hasday
Senior Production Editor: Lisa Chippendale
Publishing Coordinator: James McAvoy
Project Editor: Becky Durost Fish
Cover Design and Digital Illustration: Keith Trego

Cover Photos: front cover: AP/Wide World Photos; back cover:
Archive Photos

The Chelsea House World Wide Web site address is
http://www.chelseahouse.com

First Printing

1 3 5 7 9 8 6 4 2

Library of Congress Cataloging-in-Publication Data

Bonner, Mike, 1951–
    Paul Kariya / Mike Bonner.
        p. cm. — (Ice hockey legends)
    Includes bibliographical references (p.) and index.
    Summary: A biography of the Japanese-Canadian hockey
player who is the high-scoring forward for the Mighty Ducks
of Anaheim.
    ISBN 0-7910-5015-7
    1. Kariya, Paul, 1974– —Juvenile literature. 2. Hockey
players—Canada—Biography—Juvenile literature. 3. Mighty
Ducks of Anaheim (Hockey team)—Juvenile literature.
[1. Kariya, Paul, 1974– . 2. Hockey players.] I. Title.
II. Series.
GV848.5.K37B66 1998
796.962'092—dc21   98-31354
[b]   CIP
                                                            AC

CONTENTS

KARIYA TAKES OVER

As soon as Paul Kariya saw Teemu Selanne snare a loose puck, the Mighty Ducks' left wing knew exactly what to do. Drawing on his explosive speed, Kariya streaked toward the goal of the Phoenix Coyotes.

Selanne's pass went up in the air and bounced. Kariya evaded a Phoenix defender and caught the puck neatly on his hockey stick, then fired it at the Phoenix goal. Kariya's sizzling slapshot flew across the ice while the spectators held their breath.

The puck zipped just inside the right corner of the net behind Phoenix goalie Nikolai Khabibulin. SCORE! Paul Kariya's shot won the game by a score of 3–2. Kariya's teammates held their sticks high and mobbed the talented left winger.

The date was April 27, 1997. The Mighty Ducks had evened the playoff series in sudden-death overtime. Among the first to congratulate Kariya

Friends on and off the ice, Paul Kariya (left) and Teemu Selanne confer during a game.

was Selanne, his close friend both on and off the ice. Kariya would be credited with his fifth 1997 National Hockey League playoff goal. Finnish-born Selanne would get credit for an assist.

Having won this game, the Mighty Ducks of Anaheim were tied at three games apiece with the Phoenix Coyotes. The seventh and final game would be played at the Ducks' home in Anaheim. They were usually at their best in front of the 17,651 screaming fans in sold-out Arrowhead Pond.

To reach this point, the Ducks had come a long way in a short time. This was only the franchise's fourth year of play. Owned by the Disney company, the franchise had taken its name from the 1992 Disney motion picture *The Mighty Ducks.* In the movie, actor Emilio Estevez leads a group of kids to success in a hotly contested junior hockey competition. Along the way, both Estevez and the kids learn a lot about what it takes to win in athletics. They also discover that qualities like honesty and compassion are even more important than the final score in a game. The popularity of the multimillion-dollar movie ensured the release of two Mighty Ducks sequels, in 1994 and 1996.

In the meantime, the Disney organization had created its real-life hockey team, with colorful uniforms of purple, jade, silver, and white. The team symbol of a duck-shaped hockey mask set over a pair of crossed sticks helped give the young Southern California club an identity. In their first three seasons the Ducks posted losing records—typical for an expansion team. Finally, in 1996–97, they improved to 36–33–13, finishing fourth in the NHL Western Conference and earning a berth in the playoffs.

Professional oddsmakers figured the Mighty Ducks were fortunate to have come this far, and nobody besides rabid Anaheim hockey fans expected the Ducks to go beyond the first playoff round. True, the Mighty Ducks had been transformed from a below-average team by the timely additions of Kariya and Selanne. Still, hockey insiders felt that the young Ducks squad was at least a couple of years away from being a serious contender for the championship trophy, the Stanley Cup.

Besides, the skeptics noted, the Mighty Ducks' star left winger, Paul Kariya, was starting the series with an abdominal injury that normally would have kept him out of the lineup. Kariya stands less than six feet tall and weighs only 175 pounds—one of the smallest, lightest players on the Ducks' roster. During the 82-game regular season, Kariya's body had taken a terrific pounding. "I'm not skating at 100% right now," Kariya told the *Los Angeles Times* in early April. "I can still get around, but a quick burst, that's hard. I can skate in straight lines fine."

Paul Kariya's teammates mob him after he scores the winning goal for the Anaheim Mighty Ducks in a sudden-death playoff game on April 27, 1997.

Slight of frame, Kariya often takes a pounding on the ice—in this case, courtesy of Phil Housley (left) and Zarley Zalapski of the Calgary Flames.

Nevertheless, Kariya and his teammates were determined to prove the doubters wrong. The Ducks had lost only three times in their last 23 games. Coach Ron Wilson, considered a hockey wizard by the press, encouraged his team, telling them that they stood a good chance for the championship. "Any team that finishes in the top 10 can win the Cup," the quotable Wilson told *Times* reporter Robyn Norwood on April 16. "Florida finished four in its conference last year and went to the finals."

From the start, the seven-game series with the Phoenix Coyotes was an up-and-down affair. The Mighty Ducks won the first two games handily, defeating the Yotes 4–2 each time. Kariya was outstanding in those games, collecting two of the Ducks' eight goals.

The fading Coyotes decided they had to change tactics. They concentrated on keeping Kariya and right wing Selanne away from the net. The change worked. Games 3, 4, and 5 were all losses for the Mighty Ducks. After the first period in Game 3, Kariya was shut out. In Games 4 and 5 he failed to score a goal.

The Coyotes were now leading the series 3–2, and all they had to do was win once more at home, in Phoenix's America West Arena. Road roommates Paul Kariya and Teemu Selanne talked about the problems they faced in trying to beat Phoenix. To the media, Selanne reported that Kariya knew what had to be done and was planning to do it. He said Kariya was hungry to win.

In the locker room beforehand, Coach Wilson told his worried club to lighten up. He asked them to remember how the characters in the movie *The Wizard of Oz* solved their problems. The Cowardly Lion, the Tin Man, and the Scarecrow had turned their weaknesses into strengths when it counted most.

Perhaps a movie was appropriate inspiration for this team. After a scoreless first period, Kariya and Brian Bellows combined for a pair of second-period goals to give the Ducks a 2–0 lead. But in the third period the Ducks faltered. Coyote left winger Darrin Shannon shot the puck past sprawling Ducks goalie Guy Hebert. Then, with just under

18 minutes left in regulation play, Keith Tkachuk scored for the Coyotes on a power play.

As time expired, the Ducks and the Coyotes were tied. In the playoffs, unlike the regular season, NHL rules require a sudden-death overtime. Momentum was on the side of Phoenix going into the extra period, and more than 16,000 pom-pom-waving Phoenix fans in the America West Arena were ready to celebrate.

But just as in a Hollywood-scripted movie, the stage was set for Paul Kariya's overtime heroics. Right from the faceoff, the Ducks swarmed the Phoenix net, forcing the overworked Phoenix goalie to make save after save. On the other side of the rink, Guy Hebert made two critical saves.

As the overtime period dragged on, the hard-fighting Ducks picked up the Phoenix forwards and countered their pressure with rugged physical contact. For the first time since the second period, the Ducks played like a team on a mission. When Teemu Selanne collared a loose puck in the zone, Phoenix defenseman Gerald Diduck tried to knock it away before it reached Kariya.

No such luck for Diduck. Instead, a speeding Kariya beat Diduck and smacked the puck from a spot near the left faceoff circle. The Phoenix goalie reached for it and missed. As the Mighty Ducks celebrated, the disappointed Phoenix fans headed to the exits.

Two days later, the Mighty Ducks capped the series at home with a 2–0 victory in the seventh game. Not only had they made the playoffs for the first time, they had advanced to the NHL Western Conference semifinals.

After Paul Kariya's dramatic overtime goal in Game 6, he stood in the middle of a crowd of reporters and talked about his performance. "A big, big goal," Kariya said. "I haven't played that well in the series. It was nice to get a little redemption today."

Right winger Teemu Selanne chimed in with praise for his favorite left winger: "Tonight was a good example of how hard Paul wants to compete and score big goals."

But the biggest praise for Kariya came from a newly acquired Ducks defenseman, J. J. Daigneault. The veteran Daigneault had played with the great Mario Lemieux in Pittsburgh during the Penguins' glory years. "It's time for Paul Kariya to take over," Daigneault said. "He's going to be one of the superstars for years to come."

All across North America, fans of professional hockey nodded their heads in agreement.

AMATEUR HOCKEY STAR

Future NHL hockey superstar Paul Kariya was born into a mixed-race, Japanese-Canadian family on October 16, 1974. The second of five children, Paul grew up in the rain-washed Pacific Coast city of Vancouver, British Columbia.

Founded by lumbermen and farmers in the 1860s, Vancouver is now one of the largest cities in Canada, with more than half a million people. From the beginning, the city has attracted diverse groups of settlers. Even today, Vancouver remains a major port of entry for people moving to the Americas from Asia.

Paul's Japanese father, Tetsuhiko, and his Scottish mother, Sharon, are among the many Eurasian couples who call this beautiful city home. Tetsuhiko—called "T.K." by everyone in the family—was a rugby star at the University of British Columbia, and he later earned a master's degree from the University of Oregon. When Paul was a

The 19-year-old Paul Kariya raises his stick after scoring a goal for Canada—the first of a hat trick—during the 1994 World Hockey Championships.

youngster, both T.K. and Sharon worked as school-teachers. T.K., in fact, taught mathematics and computer science at Argyle Secondary, the Vancouver high school Paul attended.

But the tolerant atmosphere that Vancouver enjoys is a recent thing. Responding to public fears during World War II, the Canadian government sent 23,000 Japanese Canadians to internment camps. T.K. was born in one of them, the Greenwood camp. The Canadian government has since admitted it did wrong, and in 1988 it issued payments as partial compensation. Paul Kariya was 14 years old when his family's reparation check arrived.

Although the Kariya family had suffered as much as other people of Japanese descent living in Canada, Paul's grandparents, Isamu and Fumiko Kariya, refused to nurse a grudge. "My grandmother never went into details about what it was like in the camp," Paul's older sister, Michiko, told *Sports Illustrated* in 1998. "But there was no bitterness on my grandparents' part. They were never bitter, never accusatory."

By the time Paul was born, the Kariya family was clearly as Canadian as maple leaves and Mounties. The bustling Kariya household featured an active and happy family life. Besides Michiko and Paul, there were soon three younger siblings, Steven, Martin, and Noriko Ann.

Throughout his youth, Paul paid close attention to his schoolwork. With a pair of dedicated teachers for parents, he knew the value of an education. In elementary school and later at Argyle Secondary School, Paul proved to be a top student. Kariya's family also taught him to be respectful and polite toward the people he met. Since then, he has always been known as a good person and a solid citizen.

For Paul, another big part of growing up was playing sports like golf, baseball, lacrosse, basketball, and hockey—especially hockey. It is difficult to exaggerate the importance of ice hockey for Canadians. Since the 1870s, when British soldiers brought their field hockey game to the frozen lakes and ponds of Canada, ice hockey has become hugely popular throughout the country—like U.S. baseball, football, and basketball rolled into one. It was Canadian governor Lord Stanley who commissioned a special silver cup to recognize the best team in the sport. To this day, National Hockey League teams compete to win the prize now known as the Stanley Cup.

A pair of skates appeared on Paul Kariya's feet practically the minute he was able to walk. His family encouraged him, and soon they realized that Paul had a special aptitude for the sport. During the cold, rainy Vancouver winters, T.K. and Sharon Kariya took their eldest son to practices and games. Often this required getting up before dawn.

Hockey was important, but Paul also excelled at other sports. When he was 13 years old, he almost quit playing hockey to concentrate on golf. Fortunately for the Mighty Ducks and NHL fans, Paul chose to continue with hockey.

Once Paul began playing in organized leagues, his skills improved dramatically. By the time he was a teenager, he was recognized by all as a standout player. The family arranged for Paul to attend a year-round program in the town of Penticton, which fielded a team in the British Columbia Junior Hockey League. Many NHL stars had

Paul Kariya with the 1993 Hobey Baker Memorial Award, which he received for being the outstanding college hockey player in the United States.

spent time in the juniors with the Penticton Panthers. In Penticton, Kariya boarded with a local couple, Roberta and Jerry Stork, whose son Dean played in the same league.

By the time Paul was ready to attend college, recruiters clamored for his services. Offers poured in from schools all over North America. The thoughtful way that he handled this decision showed his early maturity. Paul studied the programs of the various colleges and universities, considering what he wanted to do both as a student and as a hockey player. He discussed his options at length with his family, especially with his mother and father.

Paul finally selected the University of Maine—a long distance from home but a good choice. Maine's hockey coach, Shawn Walsh, saw the slim, 135-pound Kariya as the key element in the Black Bears' drive to reach the National Collegiate Athletic Association (NCAA) hockey championship.

At college, Kariya buckled down to his studies and his sport. In his first year at the school, Kariya made the dean's list of top students and worked diligently with the team. He also stayed in touch with his family and continued to behave like the polite, intelligent person he had always been.

On the ice, Kariya was nothing short of awesome, scoring 25 goals and racking up 75 assists in only 39 games. Paul fit in well with talented Maine teammates like Garth Snow, Mike Dunham, Jim Montgomery, and Cal Ingraham.

The toughest opponent Kariya and the rest of the team faced during the season was Boston University (BU). Late in the season, the Black Bears took a 30–0–2 record into a showdown at their home arena. But after falling behind 6–2, the spirited BU team beat Maine by a score of 7–6. This unexpected defeat stung like the dickens.

But the tough loss to BU didn't get Kariya or the rest of the team down. As it turned out, this was the only collegiate setback Kariya experienced. The Black Bears rebounded to capture the 1992–93 NCAA hockey title, beating BU in the process.

Along with the coveted championship, Kariya received the Hobey Baker Memorial Award as the nation's outstanding college hockey player. As the first freshman to win the honor, Kariya was gracious in his acceptance speech. He praised his teammates and coach, saying the award was as much a tribute to them as it was to him personally.

The National Hockey League now came calling. On June 26, 1993, the Mighty Ducks of Anaheim selected Kariya as the fourth overall pick in the NHL draft. Kariya's performance in the NCAA regionals had strongly impressed General Manager Jack Ferreira and Assistant General Manager Pierre Gauthier.

Kariya waited over a year before signing a contract with the Ducks. He returned to Maine for a few more games, but he spent most of the 1993–94 season playing with Team Canada, preparing for and then participating in two all-important events of amateur hockey: the 1994 winter Olympic

Games and the 1994 World Hockey Championships.

Kariya's most exciting game as an amateur took place at the Olympics in Lillehammer, Norway. At the end of an exhausting tournament, Team Canada and Team Sweden faced each other for the Olympic gold medal. A furious, hard-fought game closed with a 2–2 tie in regulation.

After a grueling 10-minute overtime period, the two teams remained tied. According to the rules, the Olympic gold medal would now be awarded to the winner of a best-of-five shoot-out.

A shoot-out is a series of one-on-one plays. Some fans detest it; others see it as hockey in its purest form. Each coach selects a small number of players—five, in this case. Each player gets one shot at the opposing team's goalie. After all five players have shot, the team with more goals wins. If the teams are still tied, they move on to a second shoot-out round. Usually, one team or the other pulls ahead quickly to claim the victory. But the usual didn't happen when the Kariya-led Canadians battled the Swedes.

The shoot-out began with Kariya and Petr Nedved scoring for the Canadians. Soon Swedish stars Peter Forsberg and Magnus Svensson also scored, and the first round ended in a tie.

The tension in the Olympic rink soared. Unlike the first round, the second shoot-out round would be sudden-death. The two teams would alternate, one shot each, until somebody scored. Then the other team would have only one chance to answer.

First up was the Swedish star Svensson. He missed. Then Canada's Nedved tried and missed. The next pair of shooters came on. This was Kariya and Forsberg.

Forsberg went first, making a spectacular

move—some say a lucky move—to slip the puck under Canadian goalie Corey Hirsch's glove. Chalk one up for Sweden. Around the world, Swedes jumped for joy and supporters of Team Canada groaned.

Now it was up to Paul Kariya to save the Canadians' bacon. Kariya took the puck and skated toward the Swedish goal. Moving in, he cut tight angles with his blades, faking Sweden's Tommy Salo so perfectly that Salo flopped down on the ice like a fish out of water.

Because Kariya's shot in the first shoot-out round had come from the right, Salo expected the puck from the left. Instead, Kariya fired a forehand shot to the right corner.

The big one that got away: Kariya's final shot is stopped by Sweden's Tommy Salo, and the Swedes win the 1994 Olympic gold medal.

Kariya answers questions at a news conference during his first official visit to Anaheim in April 1994, nearly 10 months after the Mighty Ducks chose him in the NHL draft.

Luck was with the Swedes, however. Although Salo was out of position and down on the ice, he somehow managed to deflect the incoming puck, and it fell away harmlessly.

Sweden came away from the 1994 winter Olympics with a gold medal in hockey, the country's first in 74 years of competition. The Canadians consoled themselves with the silver medal.

"I had him," Kariya told the Associated Press. "I just didn't get it high enough."

Rather than dwell on the missed shot, Kariya resolved to do better in the upcoming World Championship games in Italy. Those games proved to be another major showcase for Kariya's talent. He led the Canadians to victory, racking up 5 goals and 7 assists for a total of 12 points. In the semi-finals the Canadians revenged their loss at the Olympics by beating the Swedish team 6–0 in a runaway. In the finals against the Finns, the Canadians had to endure another shoot-out, but this time they won.

Kariya took first-team All-Tournament honors at left wing, sharing the stage with such future NHL stars as Mats Sundin, Jari Kurri, and Canadian goalie Bill Ranford. Thus ended Kariya's amateur hockey career.

In the late summer of 1994, Kariya began preparing himself to play for his new professional team, the Anaheim Mighty Ducks.

THE BROKEN SEASON

Kariya's 1993 draft selection by the Anaheim Mighty Ducks wasn't an easy feat for the team to pull off. Behind the scenes, Ducks General Manager Jack Ferreira and Assistant GM Pierre Gauthier spent weeks pretending they weren't particularly interested in Kariya. Because other teams drafted higher than the Ducks, Ferreira and Gauthier worried that another team might snatch him first.

Besides Kariya, talk around the league centered on Alexandre Daigle, a high-scoring center from the Quebec Hockey League. Just hours before the draft, Daigle agreed to a $12.5-million contract with the Ottawa Senators. The contract guaranteed that Daigle would be the number one overall pick.

"Daigle is going to be a superstar," Ferreira said, secretly happy that the Ducks could now choose Kariya. Ferreira's plan worked so well that even Kariya was surprised when the Ducks selected

In his first professional season, Paul Kariya was determined to learn the nuances of NHL hockey.

him as the number four pick. Before the draft, Kariya had joked about the name "Mighty Ducks" to the news media.

After the draft, Kariya was singing a different tune. "I love the name," he told the *Los Angeles Times*. "At first, it's different, but it grows on you. It adds spice, and it's entertaining."

The Mighty Ducks Hockey Club was barely a year old when Kariya was added to the roster. For an expansion club, the Mighty Ducks had enjoyed a large measure of success during their 1993–94 inaugural season. With 33 wins, they had tied the Florida Panthers for most victories for a first-year team. The Ducks also had 19 road wins that year, the most for any new club in the history of the NHL. A rugged defense and a low penalty average had kept the Ducks in contention throughout the year.

But the Ducks still had a glaring need for a player with the ability to score from the difficult left wing position. For that, the Ducks had picked Kariya. They saw the rookie, who would not turn 20 years old until October, as their designated scoring star.

Kariya's contract with the Ducks ran for three years, paying him $6.5 million. It was just the sort of windfall that would have sent a less thoughtful young man on a wild shopping spree.

Not Kariya. He concentrated on learning the game he had to play. He knew he would be expected to perform at the very highest level of his sport. He also knew that playing professional hockey was a dream few people achieved. Kariya dedicated himself to making the most of his opportunity. Everything else would take care of itself.

One reason Kariya showed such good judgment was the sound upbringing he had received from his parents. When Ducks coach Ron Wilson and Ferreira arrived at Kariya's house to open negotiations, they sat down to dinner with the whole family. Afterward, Kariya's mother asked Paul to clear away the dishes. Even though he was on the verge of becoming a hockey millionaire, Kariya got up from the table and did what his mother asked. Wilson and Ferreira were impressed with the grace and class of the young man they had chosen.

As he got ready for his rookie season with the Mighty Ducks, Kariya stayed at the home of pediatrician Gary Frederick and his wife, Teri, in Orange, California. Kariya occupied the room recently vacated by the Fredericks' son, a graduate of San Diego State University. Kariya told *Sports Illustrated* writer Leigh

Five days after signing his contract with Anaheim, Kariya takes to the ice in training camp, looking small in comparison to the other players.

Montville why it made sense for him to move in with a family like his own: "I've never cooked," Kariya said. "I don't own any furniture. I don't have time to go looking for a condominium or a house. Living with a family was the right thing for me."

Indeed, the fast-paced world of professional hockey demanded all of Kariya's time and energy. In addition to a new city, a new coach, and new teammates, he would have to adjust to the grueling schedule of the world's top professional hockey league.

During his first exhibition game against the visiting Vancouver Canucks, Kariya scored a breakaway goal only 3 minutes and 30 seconds into the contest. When the rookie sensation made his play, the 16,600 spectators crowding Anaheim's glitzy new Arrowhead Pond burst out with a deafening cheer.

In a September 1994 exhibition game against the Dallas Stars, Kariya shows his breakaway speed.

It wasn't just Kariya's shooting that wowed the fans. They also liked his soft, crisp passes and marvelous stickhandling. Kariya's ability to sense what was going on around him seemed almost magical.

After the Vancouver game, center Bob Corkum told the *Los Angeles Times* that Kariya's early score helped spark his teammates and raise their confidence. "That was a big goal; it got us going," Corkum said. "I can tell you, there aren't too many guys in the league who are as good as Paul is right now. He's really incredible and he's only going to get better. That's the scary thing."

Kariya blended in well with his new Ducks teammates—men like Corkum, Anatoli Semenov, Peter Douris, and John Lilley. On the ice, Kariya took on the responsibility of a scorer and passer who could add goals to the team's defensive efforts. On a personal level, Kariya's easygoing personality made him popular with the other players. To keep his focus, Kariya avoided reading about games and paid little attention to his statistics. Many players claim that the only statistic they care about is whether their team wins or loses. In Kariya's case this cliché was actually true.

The presence of another rookie, Valeri Karpov, helped take some of the pressure off Kariya. By the end of the 1994 exhibition schedule, Kariya began to feel comfortable in the high-speed NHL game. Step by step, Kariya was growing into his role as left wing. He was mastering the more refined moves practiced in the NHL and developing a few of his own. Kariya proved that he was willing to work hard to raise the Ducks to a higher level.

One of the things that helped Kariya on the ice was his ability to visualize. He pictured in his mind exactly what he wanted to do in games and then went on to do it. For years Kariya had followed players like Wayne Gretzky on the popular television broadcast *Hockey Night in Canada.* They helped Kariya imagine the kind of moves he wanted to try in a game. In the case of the great Gretzky, Kariya saw a player similar to himself in physical size and talent.

Like Gretzky, Kariya looked to pass first, shoot second. He developed spin moves to get away from tight coverage. He saw where the puck was going and anticipated perfectly.

Anaheim club president Tony Tavares, who had authorized Kariya's contract, said that the team liked the way Kariya made everybody around him better. "But we don't want to put too much pressure on him at first," Tavares added. "And the team has to make an adjustment, too. They're not used to having a high-profile guy like Kariya around."

While the team worked on its adjustments on the ice, much was going on behind the scenes. Representatives of the National Hockey League were meeting in New York City with the players' union. The two sides bickered about salaries and benefits. The players wanted the poor teams in small cities to get money from the rich teams in big cities. The owners wanted big-spending teams to pay low-spending teams extra money only when they exceeded a set salary cap. To some observers, these seemed like two ways of doing the same thing, but the owners saw their plan as a way to slow salary increases.

The owners threatened to "lock out" the players and suspend all or part of the season if they didn't get what they wanted from the labor talks. On October 1, 1994, they followed through with their threat and closed up shop, postponing the start of the regular season.

The main issue behind all the negotiations was the owners' fear that if the players made too much money, they might control the sport. On the other hand, the players and their agents believed that since hockey was becoming more popular, they should receive a larger share of the revenues.

In truth, the owners of the NHL teams did not have a good reputation for being fair to the players. Many insiders said that they had kept the professional sport small for many years as a means of controlling access to the Stanley Cup.

While the men in suits dickered over money, the weeks dragged on. Kariya and the other players waited restlessly for the dispute to be settled. To stay in condition, Kariya lifted weights and skated. He also helped improve his coordination and reflex time by taking up juggling. Before long, Kariya was nearly as good at juggling as he was at other sports. He praised the mental discipline provided by the exercise, and he even mastered the trick of taking a bite of an apple while he juggled it.

It was bad luck for Kariya that he was entering the NHL at a time when labor disagreements pushed the sport itself into the background.

Harry Sinden, president of the Boston Bruins, reflects the feeling of many fans during the 1994 NHL lockout.

In February 1995, Calgary's Zarley Zalapski (left) uses one of the few effective methods for slowing Kariya when he has the puck.

Besides ruining a large part of the 1994–95 season, the prolonged lockout earned sneers from the media and built up frustration among the fans. Finally, midway through the season, the two sides reached agreement.

At last Paul Kariya was able to play his first NHL game that counted. It took place on January 20, 1995, at the old Oilers arena in Edmonton, where Gretzky had once starred. The experience of playing in Gretsky's old haunt was an emotional one for the rookie left wing. Two days later, Kariya scored his first National Hockey League goal in a game against the Winnipeg Jets.

As the shortened season continued, Kariya took some big-league licks. The more physical NHL game took its toll on the still-slight frame of the rookie star. In March, Kariya had to sit out a game because of a sore back.

The Ducks finished the lockout season with a 16–27–5 record, far out of the running for the play-offs. But Kariya's second year in the league promised to be much better.

TEAMING UP WITH TEEMU

In his second year in the NHL, Paul Kariya continued to progress, and at mid-season his fine all-around play earned him a place in the 1996 NHL All-Star Game in Boston. There, Kariya had a chance to visit with Teemu Selanne, the Winnipeg Jets' sturdy right wing. In four NHL seasons, Selanne had established himself as a scoring star, snagging the Calder Trophy as Rookie of the Year in 1992–93. During his first year in Winnipeg, Selanne had plunked in an astonishing 76 goals. Already a three-time All-Star in the NHL, the Finnish-born Selanne was a product of the Jokerit hockey club in the European leagues.

Selanne and Kariya hit it off immediately. Kariya had always been an avid fan of such hockey greats as Wayne Gretzky, Brett Hull, Eric Lindros, and Mario Lemieux. He happily discovered that Selanne was also an unabashed fan of the superstars. Seeing their heroes up close, Kariya and Selanne became as excited as little kids. Later they told

All-Star in the making: Kariya drives past the Oilers' Ryan Smyth in December 1995.

Los Angeles Times writer Robyn Norwood that they could hardly contain themselves during Mario Lemieux's introduction. "Do you think he'd give us his autograph?" they asked each other.

When the game began, Kariya and Selanne took the ice for the NHL West All-Star team. The East built up a comfortable 4–1 lead, but saw the advantage quickly evaporate. Keyed by Kariya and Selanne, the West team fought back, scoring three times in the second period. Kariya capped this outburst with a great shot that made the score 4–3.

The East hung on gamely, protecting its lead with brilliant goaltending by Dominik Hasek. With three and a half minutes to go, however, Selanne beat Hasek to tie the score at 4.

Now it was anybody's game. But the West relaxed, thinking the game was heading into overtime. In a dramatic finish, Ray Bourque of the East found the net with only 38 seconds left. Kariya, Selanne, and the rest of the West went home disappointed. If the West had won the game, Kariya would probably have been named the Most Valuable Player.

Shrugging off the loss, Kariya returned to Anaheim, raving about Selanne's playmaking to anyone who would listen. As the regular season resumed, the Mighty Ducks' front office pondered the team's situation. Despite a poor start, the team seemed to have potential. A big problem was that players on other clubs were ganging up on Kariya. Everybody knew that he was the Ducks' main scoring threat. To win a playoff berth, the team would need someone else to occupy the opposition's defense.

Like Kariya, the Ducks' decision-makers had been impressed by Selanne's play in the All-Star

Canucks goalie Corey Hirsch blocks a Kariya shot with his stick. The Mighty Ducks' problem in the first half of the 1995–96 season was the lack of another scoring threat to complement Kariya.

Game. They especially liked the chemistry that had developed between Kariya and Selanne. How well, they wondered, might Kariya and Selanne perform together during a playoff drive? They got in touch with Selanne's team, the Winnipeg Jets.

Up north, the Jets were playing their last season in Canada. The club planned to relocate to Phoenix and change its name to the Coyotes in time for the 1996–97 season. Although Selanne was leading the club with 24 goals and 48 assists, the Jets' management decided the time was right for a trade. The Jets sent him to Anaheim with Marc Chouinard in return for defenseman Oleg Tverdovsky and center Chad Kilger.

The decision to acquire Selanne from the Jets paid off almost immediately for the Mighty Ducks. Selanne scored a goal against the New York Islanders in his first game as a Mighty Duck the following Saturday. Although the Ducks lost the game, 4–3, they had found someone who could take the focus off Kariya. Selanne was every bit as dangerous. He could make an assist or score off the breakaway as well as Kariya. No longer could the other teams double up on the left wing without paying a heavy price.

Selanne left the team for one game in February to attend the birth of his son, but was back in uni-

Teemu Selanne celebrates in April 1996 after assisting on a goal by Kariya. Together, the Ducks scoring duo sparkled, but the Ducks just missed the playoffs.

form when the Ducks met their bitter in-state rival, the San Jose Sharks. Selanne exploded in that Sharks game, recording his ninth career hat trick. (A hat trick occurs when a player scores three goals in a game. The expression comes from soccer but also applies to hockey.)

The race for a National Hockey League playoff berth tightened in March 1996. Along the way, Selanne pulled off still another hat trick in a home game against the St. Louis Blues. The Blues had Wayne Gretzky with them, but the old master managed only a single assist in the game. Kariya and Selanne crisscrossed over the ice, befuddling Gretzky's Blues en route to a 5–1 victory. Now the Ducks were within a whisker of the Winnipeg Jets for the final playoff spot in the Western Conference.

Meanwhile, every aspect of Kariya's game had been sparkling since the addition of Selanne to the lineup. Kariya was on his way to a 50-goal, 108-point season. He would also win the Lady Byng Trophy, awarded to the player who best combined playing ability with sportsmanship.

Unfortunately, the Ducks' poor start doomed them. When the 1995–96 regular season closed, the Ducks and Winnipeg were tied for the last playoff berth at 78 points. But Winnipeg had one more victory than the Ducks, finishing the year with a record of 36–40–6 compared to Anaheim's 35–39–8. As a result, the Jets went to the playoffs, and the Ducks went home.

Despite the playoff near-miss, hockey fans in Anaheim looked forward to the next season. They were eager to see how well the Kariya-Selanne combination would work in the upcoming campaign.

PLAYOFF DRIVE

Paul Kariya began the much-anticipated 1996–97 season with an injury. A nagging abdominal strain forced him to sit out the first 11 games.

That season, other impact players like Eric Lindros also missed substantial numbers of games because of injury. The NHL, in search of a villain, found three in the form of poor ice conditions at Anaheim's Arrowhead Pond, Philadelphia's Spectrum, and New York's Madison Square Garden. Rough and uneven ice at these arenas could cause injuries to a player's midsection by pulling the muscles involved in speed skating. Fast skaters were more vulnerable to the injury than others. The league office took steps to educate the teams on ways to improve ice conditions.

Abdominal pain or not, Kariya was back on the ice in game 12, determined to help his team. The Kariya-Selanne connection caught fire once more, and soon the fans were given a taste of what the

In the 1996–97 season, Kariya led the Mighty Ducks to unexpected success in the playoffs.

pair could accomplish during their first full year together.

Ever since the Mighty Ducks' debut as a team, they had served as personal punching bags for the Detroit Red Wings. In Anaheim's first home game, back in October 1993, the Red Wings had pounded the expansion Ducks, 7–2, and things had not improved much since then. As of November 1996, the Red Wings' record against the Ducks stood at 9–0–3.

Thus, when the Red Wings took an early lead in a game shortly before Thanksgiving 1996, a replay seemed in store. But this time it was going to be different. The critical moment came with the Ducks trailing 1–0 in the second period. Red Wing Darren McCarty leveled Mighty Ducks defender Bobby Dollas with a clean, hard check.

Play stopped while trainers tended to the woozy Dollas. The Ducks used the time to decide what they would do when play resumed. On the ensuing faceoff, Red Wings rookie Aaron Ward's shot was blocked. Sensing an opportunity, Kariya collared the loose puck and sent Selanne on a high-speed breakaway. The home crowd cheered wildly as Selanne scored his 13th goal of the young season.

Mighty Duck Garry Valk then scored the go-ahead goal with an assist from Ken Baumgartner, an NHL veteran playing in his 500th game. Although the Red Wings countered with a blizzard of shots at Ducks goalie Guy Hebert, the final score read 3–1 Anaheim. The Mighty Ducks had beaten the Detroit Red Wings, one of the best teams in the NHL, for the very first time!

The Ducks celebrated, and no one was happier than Kariya. More good news came on January 10. In a 5–2 win over the Buffalo Sabres at

Kariya controls the puck in a game against the New York Islanders in February 1997. With Kariya leading the way, the Ducks surged in the final months of the season.

the Pond, Kariya recorded his first NHL hat trick, scoring the last of his three goals in the third period on a power play.

Together, Kariya and Selanne led the Ducks on a surge into the last few months of the season. The Ducks also received strong contributions from players like Steve Rucchin, who was quietly on his way to accumulating 67 points on 19 goals and 48 assists. But Kariya's value to the Mighty Ducks was especially apparent. By February, with Kariya in the lineup, the Ducks had posted a 21–18–4 record. With Kariya absent, their record was 1–10–2.

Like the previous season, this one came down to the wire. On April 4, 1997, the Ducks at last secured a playoff spot with a rugged 3–2 home win over the Dallas Stars. On April 11 the Ducks completed the regular season with a 4–3 victory over the San Jose Sharks. In the Sharks game, Selanne picked up his franchise-record 51st goal. Kariya added two goals of his own to push his regular-season total to 44. Selanne and Kariya finished the season in second and third place among NHL scorers, just behind Mario Lemieux.

The win over the Sharks was sweet, putting the Ducks two games over the .500 mark and handing them their first winning season. Best of all, the win clinched home-ice advantage for the Ducks in the first round of the playoffs.

Late in the 1996–97 regular season, Kariya whips a shot against the Calgary Flames.

The Mighty Ducks reached the 1997 playoffs because of their resilience and their red-hot finish. Overcoming their third bad start in three years, the Ducks had posted the third-best record in the league since November 1. Yet most hockey fans expected the fourth-seeded Ducks to have a difficult time against their first-round opponent, the Phoenix Coyotes. Moreover, Paul Kariya still suffered from abdominal pain and spent hours rolling on a giant rubber ball to strengthen his stomach muscles.

The Ducks did have a hard time against the Coyotes, but they managed to win the series four games to three. They advanced to play the Detroit Red Wings in the Western Conference semifinals.

In the Detroit series, the Ducks lost all four games, but every one of them was a dogfight. The Red Wings, a dominant team, went on to win the Stanley Cup that year. Writing in the *Hockey News* yearbook, Robyn Norwood praised the Ducks' effort: "The Ducks pushed the eventual Stanley Cup champion Detroit Red Wings to overtime in three of four games in the second round of the playoffs, which is more than the Philadelphia Flyers managed to do in the final."

The three overtime games in the Red Wings series included one double overtime and one triple overtime. The triple overtime barn burner at the Joe Louis Arena in Detroit on May 4 set a Ducks record as the longest game in team history.

Kariya was magnificent in the first game of the series, giving Anaheim an early 1–0 lead. The Red Wings fought back and took the game with goals by Sergei Fedorov and Martin LaPointe. The second game was the triple overtime thriller. Pucks flew all over the arena as Anaheim and Detroit combined for 122 shots on goal, the third highest

With a spray of ice chips, Kariya pivots past Nicklas Lidstrom during Game 4 of the Ducks' 1997 playoff series against the Detroit Red Wings. Detroit won the game and the series.

number of shots in the history of the NHL play-offs.

Game 3 saw Kariya and Selanne each score on the power play in the first period. But the Ducks' early lead over Detroit melted all too soon. Fans crowding the Pond in Anaheim saw the undaunted Red Wings struggle back from deficits of 2–0 and 3–1 to win the game by a score of 5–3. In Game 4, Brendan Shanahan of Detroit scored in the second overtime to sweep the series for the Wings.

In the playoffs as a whole, Paul Kariya amassed 7 goals and 6 assists, for a total of 13 points in

11 games. He was the highest point producer among the Mighty Ducks.

Kariya's accomplishments that season brought him a number of postseason honors. In the voting for the Hart Trophy, given to the Most Valuable Player, he finished second to goalie Dominik Hasek of the Buffalo Sabres. Even better, Kariya won the Lady Byng Trophy for sportsmanship for the second consecutive year. He was named a first-team All-Star for the playoffs and a second-team All-Star for the regular season.

In a neat mirror image of Kariya's honors, Teemu Selanne was named a first-team All-Star for the regular season and a second-team All-Star for his work in the playoffs.

CAREER CROSSROADS

Following the Mighty Ducks' successful 1996–97 season, Paul Kariya realized that he was at a financial crossroads with his contract.

To a working person, the $6.5-million deal Kariya had signed in 1994 seems like a huge sum of money just to play hockey. However, in the world of big-time professional sports, the stakes are high. A winning team with popular players can make millions for corporate owners like Disney. The owners rely on stars like Kariya to fill the arena and encourage fans to follow the team on television and radio.

Still more money is made from merchandise sales. People love wearing the garb of their favorite sports heroes. Currently, in fact, the best-selling items of professional hockey apparel are the colorful jerseys, hats, and T-shirts of the Mighty Ducks.

Now that his contract was up, the task for Kariya

During his 1997 contract dispute with the Mighty Ducks, Kariya once again donned the uniform of the Canadian national team.

and his agent, Don Baizley, was clear: During the summer and fall of 1997, they wanted to make sure that Kariya received his fair share of the money professional hockey attracted from fans.

Convincing the Disney company to agree to terms required many months of difficult negotiation. While the talks dragged on, Kariya did not play, choosing to hold out until his salary demands were met. This meant missing the opening of the 1997–98 season, which was especially painful for Kariya because the Ducks' first game was played in Tokyo against his hometown team, Vancouver.

Kariya's holdout stretched to 32 games in all. Besides Paul's keen disappointment at not being out on the ice with his teammates, the money issue took its toll on the rest of the Mighty Ducks as well. During Kariya's contract dispute, the Ducks went 11–15–6, falling behind other teams in the Western Conference. It was obvious to anyone following hockey that the Ducks needed to get the game's most dynamic player back on the ice.

It wasn't easy for Kariya to hold out. He desperately wanted to be back with his team. He stayed in touch with Selanne and several others. Finally, on December 9, 1997, the salary stalemate was broken. Kariya didn't get the three-year $27-million contract he wanted, but he did receive an attractive two-year $14-million pact.

"I'm excited and happy to be back with my teammates and the Mighty Ducks organization," Kariya said. "I'm ready to play and want to help this team win and get back to the Stanley Cup playoffs."

When he returned to the Ducks, he came to play for a new coach, Pierre Page. In late May 1997 the Disney company had fired Coach Ron Wilson, citing "philosophical differences," even though Wilson had led the Ducks to their first playoff appearance. Since then, Wilson had landed on his feet, signing a $2.1-million deal to coach the Washington Capitals in the Atlantic Division.

Regardless of the coach, it was Kariya who seemed to make the difference for the Ducks. No sooner had he returned to the ice than the Mighty Ducks again started to win games. Within a few weeks, Kariya displayed the same dazzling skills he had shown the previous season. To top things off, Teemu Selanne was also healthy and raring to go.

Defensively, the Ducks had never looked better. New coach Pierre Page felt confident that goalie Guy Hebert and the veteran defenders could hold off assaults on the Ducks' net. More important, the defensive side could get the puck out of the zone and into the hands of the forwards. By January 1998 the Ducks were collecting win after win. Despite their poor start, they had a chance to make the 1998 Stanley Cup playoffs.

Suddenly, however, disaster struck. During a nationally televised game against the Chicago Blackhawks on January 31, Kariya was hacked down after scoring his second goal.

Kariya bounced back up, but Coach Page took him out shortly afterward. Kariya complained of a headache, and soon he was diagnosed with a serious concussion, the fourth of his career.

Television replays showed that Kariya had taken an expertly aimed stick to the jaw from Blackhawk Gary Suter the instant after he flipped the puck into Chicago's net. Although the broadcasters announcing the game agreed that Suter probably should have been whistled for a foul, no penalty was called.

At first it was hoped that Kariya would be back in uniform before long. But as the days went by, his headaches continued. He forgot things, and irrational thoughts flitted through his mind. The doctors said that once his headaches stopped, it would take at least another month before he could be cleared to play.

Kariya never did return during the 1997–98 season. All told, with the holdout and the concussion, Kariya managed to play in only 22 games that year, scoring 17 goals and making 14 assists.

No one felt the pain of his layoff from the game more than Kariya. "I've been watching every movie made by mankind," he said in an April 1998 interview. "And 'trying' to play golf. I walk the course to get fresh air."

With Kariya unable to play, the hopes of Mighty Ducks fans vanished in a puff of smoke. The team began a downward slide that soon eliminated the Ducks from the 1998 Stanley Cup race.

Not only did Kariya's injury prevent him from participating in the team's playoff drive, it also eliminated his chance to play for Canada in the winter 1998 Olympic Games in Nagano, Japan. Asian fans had eagerly awaited the arrival of the star NHL forward of Japanese descent. When doctors informed Kariya that his concussion would keep him from the Olympics, Kariya said it was the worst day of his life.

All told, in four years of professional hockey, Paul Kariya had missed large parts of every season except one, 1995–96. Labor and money problems had been the source of some missed games. But the main culprits were the injuries that Kariya had sustained. Now it seemed that the persistent headaches resulting from his latest concussion would threaten his hockey career.

Anyone familiar with the sport knows that NHL players pay a high physical price. An early exam-

Joining the Ducks for his first practice after the contract trouble, Kariya listens to the team's new coach, Pierre Page.

ple for Kariya occurred when he was still in the British Columbia Junior Hockey League. He was on the ice for the Penticton Panthers when a stick to the chin broke four of his teeth. He had to undergo dental surgery to repair the damage.

The 1996–97 NHL season offered more such examples. At the start of the season, Kariya missed 11 games with his abdominal injury. No sooner was he back on the ice than he was decked by Toronto defenseman Mathieu Schneider. Writing for *The Sporting News*, Steve Bisheff described Schneider's hit on Kariya as a "cheap shot."

"The first few days after it happened, I was pret-

Back in the thick of it, Kariya (left) fights to stop Chris Simon of the Washington Capitals on December 12, 1997. Seven weeks later, Kariya received the concussion that threatened to end his career.

ty mad," Kariya said. "I couldn't believe how dirty it was. But what are you going to do?"

Whenever Kariya misses games because of injury, Mighty Ducks fans can expect few wins, because defenders know they can double up on Selanne. Worse, the sport as a whole suffers when Kariya is out because few other hockey players command such a large following. To the game of hockey, Paul Kariya brings style, creativity, and class.

The Kariya style could not have arrived at a better time. Slowly fading from the NHL scene are the plodding defensive games played for so many years. Previously, the usual NHL strategy had been to make sure the other side didn't score and hope for a lucky break yourself. Today, more NHL coaches are opting for the attacking style favored in Europe. There are fewer fights and penalties. Winning in this type of game depends more on finesse and skating ability than on checking and fighting. Fans love it.

The new game is better suited to players like Kariya—players who want to skate rather than fight. Since the 1980s, the NHL has tried to move away from the excessive violence that has long characterized its games. Following the 1987–88 season, for example, the NHL made an honest attempt to reduce fighting by deciding to eject players who become involved in brawls. Nevertheless, some say the penalties are still not strong enough. For his high-stick assault on Kariya's head in 1998, Gary Suter received a four-game suspension without pay and a $1,000 fine. By contrast, Kariya was deprived of his Olympic opportunity and possibly the rest of his career.

The situation is complicated, because teams often feel they need to play rough in self-defense. The game may be changing, but there is still a role for players like 1995–96 Mighty Ducks winger Todd Ewen, who racked up 1,600 penalty minutes in 10 seasons. Teams contend that players like Ewen are there to protect stars like Kariya from cheap shots and injuries—that is, to protect them as much as possible.

Aside from the chance of injury, hockey demands a lot of hard work, and Kariya has been especially noted for his dedication to the game. His daily routine includes not only practice time but also hours in the weight room, putting muscle on his lean frame. Between games Kariya also pays careful attention to his equipment. In his early days as a professional, he tried many types of sticks and experimented with their curvature. Eventually he settled on the gradually curved stick he uses today. This analytical study of his equipment is typical of his approach to the game.

Except for injuries, lockouts, and contract hassles, Paul Kariya's rise to the summit of professional hockey has been swift and sure. When *Hockey News* featured him on the cover, the magazine was confirming what many fans already knew: Paul Kariya is the most exciting hockey player around today.

Kariya's enormous popularity among fans can be measured by the number of Internet pages devoted to him—13 at last count. Memorabilia such as hockey cards and figurines that feature Kariya are also highly prized by collectors. Kariya's most significant early hockey card appears as No. 50 in the rare 1992 Upper Deck "Czech" set. This 100-card grouping of promising amateurs and draft picks has soared in value since it was first issued, with Kariya's card as the highest priced item.

Personally, despite his prominence in the public eye, Kariya prefers to live a quiet life. He enjoys home-cooked meals, and a special favorite is crab bisque, a rich cream soup made from shellfish and vegetables. Kariya developed his appetite for seafood in his hometown of Vancouver.

Interestingly, Kariya has loosened up and become a bit less private since his friend Teemu Selanne arrived in Anaheim. "Before, Paul used to be kind of a room-service guy," said Bobby Dollas in January 1998. But "Teemu goes out with the boys, and now so does Paul."

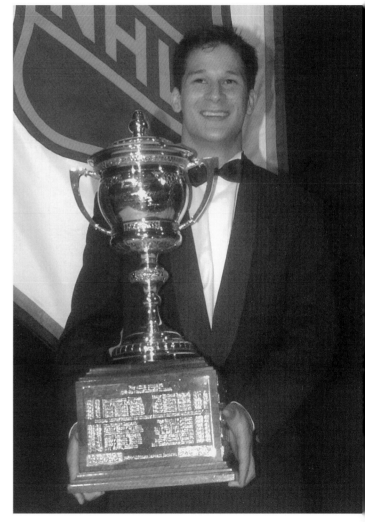

Kariya holds the first of his Lady Byng trophies, awarded for sportsmanship combined with high-quality play—a fitting tribute to a man who aspires to be a fine human being as well as a hockey star.

Meanwhile, the well-spoken Kariya finds himself making public appearances, doing promotions, and acting in TV commercials. He is frequently interviewed by the media, and not always about hockey. Kariya's most famous TV spot is the pea-shooting ad he did to promote hockey as "The Coolest Game on Earth."

Although Kariya became a hockey millionaire at age 19, he told *Boy's Life* writer John McManus that he still believes a good education means more than hockey. "It's difficult to do anything without a college education," Kariya said. "Education is the most important thing. Hockey's been good to me financially, but in terms of handling your money or being a successful person, it's important to have that education."

This son of schoolteachers has also demonstrated his concern for society, wanting to share some of what he has received with the less fortunate. On February 15, 1998, Kariya donated over $2 million from his hockey contract to 28 Anaheim-area charities. The money went to groups that try to stop domestic violence, ensure adequate health care for children, and provide hospital services to the poor.

If injuries do not prematurely end his career, Kariya may go on to become one of the greatest stars in the history of hockey. As a player, he shows constant creativity and inventiveness. The soft touch he has with his stick allows him to make shots and passes that astound even veteran coaches and players who think they have seen it all.

But no matter how good he is on the ice, it is as a human being that Paul Kariya is most successful. His generosity and sense of purpose are rare among people in any profession, not just athletics.

"The biggest thing for me is to be remembered as a good person," Kariya told *Hockey Book* reporter Cammy Clark in a 1998 interview. "Of course, you'd love to have won the Stanley Cup, but a lot of factors go into that. I'd like to be remembered mostly as a good person."

Hockey fans will never have any trouble thinking of Paul Kariya as anything less than that.

Statistics

College

Season	Team	GP	G	A	PTS	PIM
1992–93	Univ. of Maine	39	25	75	100	12
1993–94	Univ. of Maine	12	8	16	24	4
Totals		51	33	91	124	16

National Hockey League

Season	Team	Regular Season					Playoffs				
		GP	G	A	PTS	PIM	GP	G	A	PTS	PIM
1994–95	Ana	47	18	21	39	4	—	—	—	—	—
1995–96	Ana	82	50	58	108	20	—	—	—	—	—
1996–97	Ana	69	44	55	99	6	11	7	6	13	4
1997–98	Ana	22	17	14	31	23	—	—	—	—	—
Totals		220	129	148	277	53	11	7	6	13	4

GP	games played
G	goals scored
A	assists
PTS	points (goals plus assists)
PIM	penalties in minutes

CHRONOLOGY

1974   Paul Kariya born on October 16 in Vancouver, British Columbia.

1980   Joins first hockey league at age 6; begins moving up through amateur ranks; becomes devoted fan of Wayne Gretzky.

1990–92   Stars for Penticton in the British Columbia Junior Hockey League; plays for Canadian Junior Team in World Games.

1992–93   Attends University of Maine, where he plays on NCAA championship team, winning the Hobey Baker Award as the country's outstanding collegiate hockey player.

1993   Selected by Anaheim Mighty Ducks as first-round draft choice and fourth overall pick.

1994   Signs a contract to play for the Mighty Ducks.

1995   Plays first NHL game on January 20 at Edmonton.

1996   Appears in first NHL All-Star Game; scores a goal and an assist; wins Lady Byng Trophy for sportsmanship.

1997   Scores first hat trick of career in game against Buffalo; runner-up for NHL MVP; wins Lady Byng Trophy for second year in a row; later in the year, holds out for first 32 games of 1997–98 season in a contract dispute.

1998   Suffers a concussion in a game against the Chicago Blackhawks on January 31 and is out for the rest of the season.

FURTHER READING

Fischler, Stan. *Strange But True Hockey Stories.* New York: Cowles, 1970.

Goodman, Michael E. *Anaheim Mighty Ducks.* Mankato, Minn.: Creative Education, 1996.

Hollander, Zander. *The Complete Encyclopedia of Hockey.* Detroit: Gale Research, 1993.

The Mighty Ducks Home Page. http://www.mightyducks.com/.

Rosenbaum, Dave, editor. *Hockey Stars Presents The Hockey Book.* Ambler, Pa.: London, 1997.

Scichili, Rob. *The 1997–98 Mighty Ducks Media Guide.* Anaheim, Calif.: Anaheim Mighty Ducks, 1997.

Staff of *The Hockey News. The Hockey News 1997–98 Yearbook.* Toronto: Transcontinental Sports Publications, 1997.

ABOUT THE AUTHOR

Mike Bonner has written about sports and sports memorabilia for *Oregon Sports News, Sports Collectors Digest, Beckett Vintage Sports, Sports Cards Gazette,* and *Sports Map* magazine. From 1992 to 1993, he wrote a column about football cards for *Tuff Stuff* magazine. His 1995 book *Collecting Football Cards: A Complete Guide* is available from Krause Publications of Iola, Wisconsin. Bonner's other works include *Shawn Kemp* in the Chelsea House Basketball Legends series. A graduate of the University of Oregon, he is married to the former Carol Kleinheksel and has one daughter, Karen.

PICTURE CREDITS: AP/Wide World Photos: pp. 22, 27, 28, 34, 37, 54–55, 57; H. DiRocco/Bruce Bennett Studios: p. 44; A. Foxall/Bruce Bennett Studios: p. 46; J. Giamundo/Bruce Bennett Studios: pp. 6, 43; Courtesy, Mighty Ducks of Anaheim: p. 40; Courtesy, Mighty Ducks of Anaheim/photo by John Cordes: p. 24; © Monty Rand Photography: p. 18; L. Redkoles/Bruce Bennett Studios: p. 2; Reuters/Chris Helgren/Archive Photos: p. 14; Reuters/Gary Hershorn/Archive Photos: p. 21; Reuters/Sam Mircovich/Archive Photos: pp. 10, 32, 38, 53; Reuters/Patrick Price/Archive Photos: p. 48; Reuters/Mike Segar/Archive Photos: p. 31; Reuters/Jeff Topping/Archive Photos: p. 9.

INDEX